T0128107

TRANSPARENT
Moments

"The Mini Book"

Lessons Learned from Life's Painful Experiences

By LaToya Reneé Jones
Edited By Dominique Lambright

authorHOUSE®

AuthorHouse™
1663 Liberty Drive
Bloomington, IN 47403
www.authorhouse.com
Phone: 1 (800) 839-8640

© 2018 LaToya Reneé Jones. All rights reserved.

No part of this book may be reproduced, stored in a retrieval system, or transmitted by any means without the written permission of the author.

Published by AuthorHouse 05/04/2018

ISBN: 978-1-5462-3653-5 (sc)
ISBN: 978-1-5462-3654-2 (e)

Library of Congress Control Number: 2018904257

Print information available on the last page.

Any people depicted in stock imagery provided by Getty Images are models, and such images are being used for illustrative purposes only. Certain stock imagery © Getty Images.

This book is printed on acid-free paper.

Because of the dynamic nature of the Internet, any web addresses or links contained in this book may have changed since publication and may no longer be valid. The views expressed in this work are solely those of the author and do not necessarily reflect the views of the publisher, and the publisher hereby disclaims any responsibility for them.

Contents

Acknowledgments

Before you begin to read this part of my book, please understand, if I begin to list EVERYONE who has impacted my life, this section of the book will be as long as my body of work. So, this is what I'm going to do. I'm going to recognize the people who have solely contributed to this project. A full list of heartfelt expressions that includes the people that I carry in my heart will be in the full completed book (I promise). Hopefully, this will add suspense and encourage you to purchase the next book to see who I listed (smile).

My family I share DNA with:
Mom's side – The Jones and Reese family
Dad's side – The Craft family, especially my brother James (Jimmy) and Cheryl Johnson
The Taylor and Hopgood families

My church, spiritual, and support families:
World Outreach Center
Be Great Ministries – Anita Clinton
Writer's Unblocked – Arnitta Holliman

Special Acknowledgements

My everything! My Lord and Savior Jesus Christ is my life in its totality. You are the reason for my existence and the reason why this book exists. I love You and want the world to know that You are my God.

My husband:

Mr. Johnny Jones, you gave me room to make my dream a reality without feeling threatened or intimidated. You are my favorite man alive and I love you. Thank you for encouraging and giving me space to birth this third baby. I love you.

My girls:

Niyah Denise, you are my firstborn and the main reason I believe in miracles. I push myself so you can see, "If Mama can do it, you can too." I love you so much and no one can take your place in my heart.

Kadence Shalom, you are my grand finale and the reason why life is sweet. In the short amount of time you have been on earth, I have so many sweet memories of you. Your energy and spunk helps to keep me young. I love you baby.

My sisters:

Sandra "Kay", Rebia, and Marlena, thank you for being the best big sisters on earth. Life is easier to live knowing that I always have your love, protection, and support. I love, appreciate, and thank you so much.

My niece:

Rochelle Taylor, thank you for your talent and setting the standard for my concept design that everyone had to measure up to. You rock!

Toni Pharm, you were unselfish with your resources, connections, and answered the abundance of questions I had about the process you were a forerunner in. I can't thank you enough. Thank you for over twenty-seven years of friendship. I love you bestie.

Wanda Booker and Wanda Jones, you have been my mentors and support system since my teen years. Thank you for your words of wisdom, insight, prayers, and loving me unconditionally. You have always seen the potential in me and you will always love and value you for that.

My Pastors:

Ervin "Skip" Henderson, you gave me permission to release what's in me by letting me know, "You don't need my permission to be great." That statement empowered and gave me the fuel tell my story with boldness just like you. Thank you for being you.

Melva Henderson, thank you for your input, direction, and showing me how to have a true servant's heart. It's impossible to place a value on the priceless deposit you have made in my life. You are the wind that I needed to Soar in the air. I love and appreciate you.

Soar Mentorship Program's mentors, big sisters, and classmates, thank you. The meetings, flying instructions, and grooming lessons conditioned me to glide through the air.

Karen Bradley and Dominique Lambright, thank you for help, and helping to make me look good.

Dedication

This book is dedicated to the woman whose legacy is my cloak of honor. By watching you my whole life, I thought breaking barriers was easy. You made it look that way, because your drive and work ethic was nothing short of amazing. I'm still reaching to achieve how you managed life in general. But you gave me a great foundation and example to build on. Thank you for passing me the great things you are made of including your dimples. Not only are you my inspiration, but you are also my angel, and most important my Mother. Oh, how I wish you were here to see the fruit of your labor and so I can hear you say, "Hot Dog, I knew you could do it; I told you none of my children were average". This is in honor of you, Boss Lady.

Everlena Taylor
January 30, 1941 – September 19, 2014

I love and miss you beyond Word's description.

Introduction

No matter what creed or nationality you are, or when you were born, there is one thing you have in common with all or at least the majority of humanity. Neither financial nor marital status play a factor in what binds you together with practically every person on the planet in this aspect. In a world where so many things separate and divide us, there are only a few things that we can all agree on that connects the totality of us as a human race. Here it is. Like me, at some point in your life, you have gone through a painful experience.

The painful experience could have been physical, emotional, mental, or any combination of the three. Some of you may have skated through those moments unscathed and moved forward without giving them a second thought. But again, like me, most of you can't say the same. Generally speaking, most if not all, painful experiences leave a lasting impression or mark that scars us for life. But, do we have to stay in that place of despair, brokenness, or heartache? Is there a way to learn to make ALL things work together for our good? Can the outcome be a positive one instead of shipwreck and hurt?

In my personal journey with this four-letter word called "pain", I've learned a few things that have helped me to more effectively navigate through many of life's challenges. If you sit back and honestly examine your own experiences, there are teachable moments, or pieces of wisdom that could make you a better person as a result of what you have endured. Not only can your story make you a better person, but it will also help someone else along their life journey.

This is why I'm opening my life to share the intimate, "Transparent Moments" from some painful things I've gone through with you. Looking back at the experiences in hindsight, not only did I learn a lot about myself and life in general, there are some things I would've done differently if I had the opportunity to turn back the hands of time. I pray you can take my life-changing experiences and learn from them, so you will not have to learn some of life's lessons the hard way like I had to. As you begin to read, I pray you are inspired, enlightened, and you're left wanting more stories like the ones you are about to read.

This mini serious is an example of what will be released in a full thirty-day devotional, along with a series of books that will focus on various subjects. I desire to see you walk in the True Freedom that God has promised. I encourage you to see yourself through my life reflections and make the adjustments that will make you a better person. Please be assured that I'm not in denial. I know I am still growing on this life journey. Hopefully, we can make a connection, so we can continue through life helping each other. Will you join me?

SECTION ONE

An Unexpected Crisis

Life Reflection One

I happily laid in my own bed for the first time since being awakened out of my sleep with unbearable pain that sent me to the hospital a week earlier. My mind replayed all of the events that happened, and I was blown away by what I had just experienced. What I went through was dramatic to say the least, along with the recovery process. However, I was grateful for being saved from the "what ifs, could haves, and should haves" that I dodged on that fateful day. More important, I'm thankful that God intervened so I could share this story.

My plans for that day included attending a dear friends' women's conference that morning. I was on the program to do the opening prayer and assist at the altar to pray for the attendee's needs. Afterward, I was going to the beauty salon to work as I do every Saturday, since I'm a hairdresser by trade. My husband, who normally doesn't work weekends, decided to pick up some overtime that day and left our two girls and me at home. Before he left, I started experiencing a lot of discomfort, so he suggested that I take some pain medicine and lay down for a little while. I agreed to it, so he handed me a glass of water with some over the counter tablets and went about his day. After he left, the pain began to increase to the point that I forgot about the pills and fell asleep to escape the pain without taking them.

When my alarm went off, I attempted to get out of bed as usual, but my stomach was hurting beyond word's description. I tried to put on a brave face for my baby's sake, but the pain was overwhelming. I curled up in a fetal position and sobbed uncontrollably. Petrified to see their mother in that condition, my oldest girl had a complete meltdown, while my little one pleaded with me through her tears to take the medicine daddy left so the, "ouwe can go bye-bye". After a few moments, my tall baby, as I call her, managed to pull herself together and called my older sister, who showed up at my house in what seemed like two minutes, to take me to the Emergency Room.

By the time we made it to the hospital, the pain was so bad, I could barely walk so I was taken to the back right away. Since the pain was in my abdomen, the first thing they had to rule out was a possible pregnancy. Until the test came back negative, they couldn't give me any strong pain medication to soothe the level of pain I was experiencing. By then, misery was an understatement for the suffering I was enduring. Not only was the pain too much to bear, but I was also starting to get scared and wondered what all of this was about. When they finally confirmed it wasn't a baby (thank God), they began to draw multiple tubes of blood and schedule x-rays as well as other tests to get to the source of the problem. The picture from the x-ray showed there was something there. But, the image wasn't clear enough for the staff to draw a conclusion, so a CAT scan was ordered. Normally, that wouldn't have been an issue, but not in my case. I was known for having allergic reactions to the ink that's injected inside of the body to illuminate the pictures.

"How did you find out that you were allergic to the ink and what happens during an allergic reaction?" were the questions I was asked by the medical professionals. I explained to them my allergy was to the iodine in the ink. I also can't eat shellfish, I break out in itchy hives and my throat swells, making it hard to breathe. They had a meeting to discuss the matter and a strategy for me. The doctor explained that my condition was serious and possibly life-threatening. They were more concerned about the underlying problem than they were about the possibility of hives and swelling. The concern was so great, they devised a plan to inject me with the medicine I was known for being allergic to despite the risk. They knew they were taking a gamble with their decision, because of the possibility of being held liable if the outcome wasn't favorable. This was something that all of us wanted to avoid. The other medical facility I went to before this ordeal wouldn't take the chance and had it documented in my files not to perform this procedure on me. I was scared about everything that was going on. But the thought of taking the injection knowing the risk had me paralyzed in fear. The doctors assured me that before I was given the injection, I was getting three rounds of a powerful antihistamine and steroid to counteract any kind of reaction I might have as a safeguard. A team of specialists were also called to be in place and stand watch just in case the preventative measures didn't work.

Thank God, their strategy worked. The test showed that my small intestines were obstructed and had a loss of blood flow due to an incarcerated hernia. This meant, the hernia was causing damage because it was growing inward and undetected, like a hidden balloon squeezing and shifting my insides. A traditional hernia normally sticks out where it can be spotted and repaired promptly. The loss of blood was causing my intestines to die quickly. I was at risk of suffering permanent damage and having to live with a coloscopy bag. Or worse than my life being altered, I could've lost my life. Looking back, living with the bag wouldn't have been the end of the world. However, at that moment, all I could see was my life changing as I knew it. I didn't want that for myself, or for my husband and children. The doctors worked hard to keep my insides as close to normal as possible. They weren't afraid to take what they felt was a lesser risk for a greater cause. By putting a reliable system in place in the event of something tragic happening, my life as well as the quality of my life was saved.

The Lesson Learned

I admit, I'm guilty of being influenced to always play it safe. I was taught to follow the proper protocol, stick to the script, and obey the rules. Rules are like a bank of a dam that was created for my safety and the script ensures no mishaps. I agree with that, because it's better to be safe than sorry (in most cases). If you ask my clientele, they will tell you how I am a stickler for playing it safe. I am known for saying "no" to risky chemical services without hesitation. I have turned down top dollar for highlights and straighteners if there was any faint concern of damage taking place to the hair I labored over. Some of my beloved clients have been put on hair punishment, because I restricted them from getting any service that I wasn't comfortable performing. Some of them found another stylist to do the service. The vast majority of the time, they came back bearing gifts and apologies asking me to take them back as clients and revive their comatose hair.

What if Jesus always played it safe? The miracles He performed for the masses would've been cut down dramatically, if He did everything by the book of His day. If His life is taken into consideration, He repeatedly went against the grain for the greater good of advancing God's kingdom and enriching lives. Even when the people who were closest to Him didn't understand, He didn't get boxed in by letting the traditional protocol of men to stop Him from serving the greater good. Although He obeyed the laws of the land, He didn't ignore His instincts to take a more effective approach for the sake of saving others.

It's my desire for you to understand that it is OK to take a smaller risk for the sake of a greater cause. You must discern every moment you are in, weigh all sides, and then make a quality decision after praying. Don't automatically assume the answer is no, because a risk of some sort is involved. Please hear my heart. I am not giving a green light, permission, or advising you to break the civil laws of the land you live in. I am not going to bail you out of jail for stealing, killing, and destroying yourself. That also includes anyone else or any property for that matter.

When facing a situation where a hard decision must be made, stop and ask yourself the following:

What would happen if I step out on faith and not ignore what my gut is telling me to do?

Would the outcome be different if I was willing to take another approach?

Can I honestly say everything was done to remedy the situation?

Most importantly, what is God saying?

There's True Freedom in knowing that you can walk away from life's hard decisions without regret or second-guessing yourself. The greater can be waiting for you on the other side of a small risk. Is it time to find out?

Life Reflection Two

The ordeal that I went through concerning my health caught me completely off guard (sort of). Although my plans on that fateful day did not include being rushed into emergency surgery, looking back, can I truly say I was caught completely off guard? To be honest, the answer to that question is a resounding no. As I look back on all the events that led up to having two operations to save my life and intestines without prior notice, my body was giving me little hints for months prior to that day. Some of those hints came in the form of minor pains and discomfort that I medicated with over the counter remedies with the thought in mind: "I am too busy and have too many obligations to allow something trivial like a tummy ache to keep me from my daily grind." Other hints came in the form of words of concern from people that love me saying, "Are you still having stomach problems? You were dealing with that when I spoke to you last month." People were constantly telling me, "Maybe you need to go to the doctor, because something doesn't sound right." The biggest hint I ignored was my body simply saying, "LaToya, you don't feel good, stop and take care of yourself."

Although I was pressing through pain on a daily basis, I was living in misery and putting what I felt in my body on the back burner. I started taking extra fiber in every form I could get my hands on for my body that was moving at a snail's pace. This is significant, because I am the same person whose system was so on point, I have friends that were jealous of how often I went to the bathroom, as they took their vegetable laxatives hoping for a breakthrough. I had containers of an orange flavored, and sand-like substance that was mixed with water at the salon and at home. My older clients would watch me mix the concoction asking me if I remembered when they had the vanilla flavor. "You need to drink that faster, so it won't get thick in the cup." Those words still echo in my memory; they came from a client in her eighties giving me advice on how to drink this stuff. My mixed feelings didn't know if I should be embarrassed or grateful for the pointers.

Not only was I dealing with ongoing stomach issues, but I also began to have foot pain from a heel spur and a condition called Plantar Fasciitis. This is an inflammation of a thick band of tissue that connects the heel bone to the toes that caused tremendous pain. Foot problems are a hairdresser's nightmare. I walked with a terrible limp for months and was desperate for some relief, so I can keep up with my never-ending to-do list. I started going to see a podiatrist every five weeks to get cortisone injections directly in my foot. Even though the foot pain was almost debilitating, I still didn't take any time off to care for myself. I purchased some insoles and continued to work twelve and sometimes fourteen-hour days standing up.

A lot of those days I worked without a break with shooting pain that made my life pretty dismal. On top of that, my iron, serotonin, and magnesium levels were all low. My short-term memory was affected. I forgot simple daily tasks and monthly deadlines that I did out of routine for years. I forgot about client's appointments too many times to remember (no pun intended). Them, along with other people would send me text messages that I forgot to respond to. Conversations were hard to recall, and I made a lot of people mad. I didn't let anyone know I wasn't feeling well. I plowed through every day just trying to manage the heavy load.

My energy level was at an all-time low. My daughter was late going to school every day, because the thirty-minute commute to get her there by 7:30 a.m. became too much for me to handle. I already struggle with my work schedule, but it became even worse when I just didn't have the strength to get through the day. I was taking naps between clients and adapted a new coffee habit to aid me in my day. I felt terrible and the heightened sensitivity to the physical pain didn't make things any better.

The demands of working as a hairdresser to a high demand clientele, being a business owner, and an operations manager was starting to wear on me. The solace I could always rely on for my high-pressure existence was going to church. Corporate worship was a place of escape and comfort that gave me the liberty to talk and sing to God without interruption. It was a safe place to cry an ocean of tears to release the emotion that was trapped inside of me. Church was like the pressure relief valve on a hot water tank that prevented me from blowing up. But, my means of temporary diversion was intruded upon when I started having trouble balancing the multiple hats of various ministry obligations that I once wore with grace and style. It got to a point where I started to resent going to a church that I loved, because it felt like nothing more than a task-driven drudgery for me.

The demand from all of the people who depended on me, along with the pressure of being a good wife and mother was pulling from a depleted source. But, I kept it to myself and suffered in silence because I didn't want to disappoint anyone. While I'm being honest, my twenty plus year career in the beauty industry felt like a death sentence that I began to hate. I was growing increasingly hostile towards the salon and people I once adored. Why did I endure all of this madness that my life turned into? I chose to remain silent about what I was feeling physically and emotionally. I couldn't blame anyone but myself, because no one put a gun to my head to force me to do anything. Every fourteen-hour day that I worked, I made every appointment. It was me that opened my life to every person who sat in my chair or dealt with in business.

My chummy demeanor made them feel comfortable enough to call, text, inbox, or post their hair needs all over my social media pages as if they weren't aware it was well after midnight. Better yet, on the only two days out of the week I wasn't in a smock, I still didn't draw the line and make everyone respect my right to a private life. Every time I stepped in front of the microphone to minister, and every altar appeal that I took responsibility for operating at church, I did it on my own accord in spite of the pain I was in. Because of the nature of the church I attended at the time, if I would've admitted I wasn't in a good place, they would've gladly accommodated my need. So, I couldn't blame them either. The hints that I ignored earlier, became demands that I had no other option but to submit and obey. This class was taken at the school of hard knocks. But, the message was heard loud and clear.

The Lesson Learned

After coming through this ordeal, I knew it was time for me to re-evaluate my approach to life. I hope by reading my story, you might sense the need to examine your life too. Don't wait for the subtle hints you are currently ignoring to grow out of control. Most five-alarm fires start out as a small flame that can be contained and put out before it grows into an inferno that causes damage beyond repair, or recognition. If I would have simply listened to my body and gave it the attention it needed before the whisper became a loud roar, I could've avoided a lot of what I went through. It is not normal for an overall healthy person to have unexplained pain, consistent discomfort, or new symptoms pop up out of the nowhere. I'm pleading with you to not make the same error in judgment that I made. LISTEN TO YOUR BODY! You are made in God's image, so your body is a fearfully and wonderfully made temple. However, without the proper maintenance and upkeep, even the most prized structure will eventually be nothing more than a tragic display of decay and ruin. I had to stop making bad decisions like ignoring and neglecting myself and use this nightmare as a teachable moment. Hopefully, my story will encourage you to make any adjustments that need to be made to live a better life.

Whether it's physical, mental, or emotional, a lack of self-care doesn't make you more a spiritual person or a humanitarian. In fact, the very opposite occurs. Neglecting yourself makes you less effective in your daily roles, because no one is getting the best of you, including God. It also makes you a prime piece of prey to be eaten up by the devour that is lurking to steal, kill, and destroy your life as you know it. Take the time to live a balanced life by making sure you make yourself a top priority. Having boundaries and having the courage to say no isn't a bad thing.

Going to the doctor for regular check-ups will preserve the quality of your life or save it altogether.

When making changes to live better are being made, ask yourself:

Is there a healthier you waiting to live a more satisfying life?

What changes need to be made that will make a healthier lifestyle possible?

Who will benefit from a better you besides yourself?

Are you worth it?

True Freedom can be found in living a full and healthy life, as opposed to merely existing in misery from day to day. Don't put off making the changes that need to be made for you to enjoy life to the fullest. The time begins now.

Life Reflection Three

The hubster (as I lovingly call him) is a weekend homebody for the most part. He normally spends daddy/daughter time with our girls on Saturdays when I'm working. Since the three of them wake up before six in the morning on weekdays, Saturdays are deemed as their designated sleep late day. By the time they are up and about, I am usually gone or about to leave home. So, what should have been a pleasant surprise for my daughters to wake up to their mother at home on a Saturday morning, wound up being one of the worst days of their life. Since Daddy was gone, they were left feeling scared and helpless, because they had to take care of Mama instead of Mama taking care of them. Hearing their cries of fear and concern reminded me of my own childhood, I knew exactly how they felt and what they were going through.

I was nine years old when my mother had her first health crisis. She was driving home from work and blacked out, which caused her to lose control of the car. When she was rushed to the hospital, she discovered she had diabetes. That was the moment my sisters and I was introduced to the world of doctors, nurses, hospitals, and prescription medication. My mother educated and took good care of herself, so she managed to avoid the major side effects and complications like blindness, amputation, and kidney failure. But she had to deal with minor side effects that still shook me to watch as a child.

I praise God that we never had to utilize our training that we were taught in case we found her unconscious from slipping into a diabetic coma from her glucose level being too high. She also knew her body well enough to know when her "sugar" was getting too low and needed something sweet to raise her level. But as time progressed, other issues arose, and her health began to decline. She had an enlarged heart and suffered from congestive heart failure, along with several other conditions she was diagnosed with. I have vivid memories of my sisters and I watching our mother battle her way back from life-threatening circumstances so many different times. She recovered from a stroke, walking pneumonia, and surgeries of different types. In fact, it was a normal part of our routine for us to visit her in the hospital, rehabilitation facilities, and nursing homes. It became nothing to watch her take shots of insulin and a ton of medicine while always being on edge about her well-being. That was life for my family until she passed away at the age of seventy-three.

Having a childhood of constantly being worried about Mom's well-being was never an existence I wanted for my babies, because the anxiety never goes away once it's there. From my own experience, I was well into my adult years still being haunted by a phone that rang late at night. I flinched at the sound of my phone ringing, because bad news about my mother was usually on the other end of "hello". Even after her death, I continued to jump up startled when the phone rang, especially late at night after I fell asleep out of mere habit. Once I shook the sleep off to realize the calls were no longer concerning my mom, I sat on my bed and cried a river. Not only was I mourning her loss, the tears came from the emotion that I had bottled up over the years.

I wept over every time I had to watch her in agony and had to be strong by not showing any fear for her sake. I cried over the times she was reluctant to go the hospital, because she was more concerned about leaving me at home before she went grocery shopping than she was about her own health. The tears were over every time I had to reassure her that it was ok for her to go to the emergency room to take care of herself, that she didn't have to worry about me. I never knew the amount of emotional weight I was under that was connected to my mother's health that I finally released once she was at rest. Now that I'm the mother of children that had to endure the same kind of anxiety, I feel like I failed them. I struggle with regret that I created that kind of existence for them by not doing a better job of protecting them, because I neglected myself.

Besides my babies being shaken up and robbed of their peace, my sister had to drop everything and run to my rescue that fateful morning because I was in too much pain to drive. She had to make sure my children were taken care of, on top of getting me to the hospital and informing my family. Since she unofficially stepped into my mother's role as the family matriarch, she was the first person I thought of to call, because I didn't want to disturb my husband at work.

What I didn't know was my daughter called him, so he left work to be by my side. Leading up to this situation, he had already taken me to other urgent care clinics and emergency rooms for stomach pain. Because he's seen me go through two different stomach surgeries and a host of other health issues, he was shaken. He spent a lot of time in the hospital's chapel praying for me to come through the surgery. He later told me that he couldn't imagine raising our children alone and losing his wife of over twenty years at such a young age. He felt helpless, because he couldn't help me, and was scared for my well-being. To make matters worse, a couple of weeks before this incident, my husband purchased the girls and I a SUV. He put a significant amount of money on the down payment and wanted the overtime to replace our savings. Because I was on medical leave without warning, not only did he have to carry the household alone, he also had a brand-new car note to deal with by himself.

My family and close friends were also alarmed, so they and came to the hospital to see about me, as well as support my husband. A group of them was at the women's conference that I was scheduled to attend. The service started at 9:00 am and every one of them had to minister in some capacity so I know the day was long for them. It was especially long and grueling for the founder of the organization who led the service that day, and her husband who always worked behind the scenes assisting her. The surgery wasn't over until late that evening, but they stayed the entire time regardless of how tired they were. While I was being operated on, my circle (as I call them) devised an entire plan to take care of my responsibilities. My best friends rearranged their lives to help with my babies, so my husband didn't have to miss more work.

I just enrolled my oldest daughter in two summer programs. Every day for a week, my dearest sister/friend drove forty-five minutes each way for her to go to school for only three hours. When she picked her up, she dropped her off at another program. My daughter stayed with her and her three daughters during my entire hospital stay. The dear friend that held the women's conference stepped in, along with her daughter, to give my mother-in-law a break since my little one stayed with her during my hospital stay. They had my three-year-old and their baby girl who is only two months older, so there was a party at their house. My church family was sent an urgent alert to begin praying and my pastor came to visit me. He called on a regular basis and brought me a gift from the ministry. People from the congregation had to intervene to cover assignments and duties I was scheduled to fulfill at church.

All of my client's hair appointments were canceled without warning for over two months. Some of those pending appointments were for hairdos for special occasions including a major holiday. Most of them understood, but some of them were disappointed and never returned. My business responsibilities at the salon had to be put on hold. As operations manager, it's my responsibility to collect rent payments from the stylists and write out their receipts. I also keep the salon clean and purchase the toiletries and supplies. My co-worker graciously kept up the salon for me and never asked to be compensated for the inconvenience. Also, people showed up in droves to offer assistance. People that I haven't seen in years showed up at my door with needed money and food to donate to my family to help while I healed and recovered at home. I had friends send money from as far as Tennessee to show their love and support. I still get emotional when I think about everyone that came through for me, especially for my girls. I witnessed a true display of love in action that spoke volumes. However, amid all of the generosity, there was a teachable moment I walked away with.

The Lesson Learned

A lot of lives were interrupted simply because I made a bad decision to ignore my health. This ordeal became an emergency not only for me, but for almost everyone I'm connected to. The comforting love I experienced was tainted with the residue of regret and embarrassment, because I wasn't prepared for the moment I found myself in. Learn from my mistake and keep this in mind. Every decision that you make will impact somebody's life in one way or another. The more influence and responsibility you have, the more lives will be affected by what you do or decide not to do. When you don't take care of yourself or make the proper provisions by having systems in place should something ever happen to you, people are left to pick up your pieces and tie your loose ends. Be responsible and have a plan in place to take care of your personal concerns should an emergency arise.

Make sure you have some money saved, and have health and life insurance policies in place. Have a plan of action regarding your loved ones so no one will be caught off guard if anything happens to you that requires someone else to handle your daily responsibilities. Don't make others in your circle suffer by neglecting this very important part of your life. At some point, any one of you might end up in the place where life can change in the blink of an eye. God forbid if you find yourself in an emergency room scenario like I did. If you do, it's better to be prepared for life's tragedies so your mind can be at ease no matter what happens. There's True Freedom in knowing there are safeguards in place, so the ball will not be dropped, because you were caught off guard in the game of life.

SECTION TWO

A Revived Dream

Life Reflection One

I enrolled in a mentorship program that changed the course of my life, because it helps women discover the why for their existence. In fact, that program is the inspiration behind this book being released. They use a holistic approach that deals with the spirit, soul, and body so every aspect of life is impacted. During one of the classes that dealt with our soulish state of being, a question was asked that we had to write the answer to in preparation for an upcoming project. The question was simple, and it should've been easy to answer. However, it challenged me in a way that took me completely off guard. The question was, "What did you dream about as a child?"

You're probably wondering why there would be a problem in responding to something so elementary. Here's the reason. When I began to attempt to recall my childhood dreams, I couldn't remember them. I was stunned that I had no recollection of ANY of my dreams knowing that I dreamed big as a child. Feeling troubled, I put some random answer down and left class that night with this overwhelming sense of confusion and sadness. But I managed to shake off what I felt as the week progressed. The escape from the disappointment was short lived when I was faced with the same challenge in the following week's session.

A different mentor was teaching that evening on creating a vision board for our God-given purpose. As she was going through her own series of questions that she wanted us to reflect on, I was blindsided once again. All she asked was an easy two-part question, "What do you currently dream about and what keeps you up at night?" Sounds simple, doesn't it? Just like the week before, when I attempted to write a response, I was forced to face the realization that something in my life had gone terribly wrong. I drew another blank! I couldn't recall any of the dreams or aspirations that I had as a child the week before. Now, here I am as an adult with absolutely no dreams of my own to write down.

Ironically, I didn't have a problem responding the second part of her question but facing the reality of that answer was a hard pill to swallow. What kept me up at night was pushing everyone else's vision, making their dreams come true, and making sure their needs were met. I stayed up well past midnight writing agendas to meet the monthly deadlines for meetings I conducted. I stayed up at night brainstorming and praying for innovative ideas that were shot down like the effort that went into them meant nothing. I stayed up at night cleaning a business without any assistance from anyone other than my husband and daughters. I stayed up at night making sure I accommodated everyone's haircare needs although my alarm was still going to sound at 4:00 in the morning for my husband to wake up for work. My alarm is also set at 5:40 am to wake up my children for school before I go to work to hardly ever leave before nine or ten at night.

There wasn't enough room on the paper to write down the real answer to the question. Besides, I wasn't mentally prepared to admit that what kept me up at night really had nothing to do with me and my dreams. Like the week before, I put on a brave front that evening and left class with a forced smile. But, on the inside of my soul I could hear bombs going off and walls crashing down like I was in a mental war zone. At that moment, I felt robbed, violated, and worst of all, empty. I was forced to deal with the devastating reality that I had been mentally and emotionally seduced by the words of people that I trusted throughout my entire life. They subtly suggested that my dream wasn't feasible, so they steered me in a "more tangible and realistic" direction to ensure my so-called success. Over the course of a number of years, I repeatedly heard, "I let my dreams die to sow faithfully into a field of another, because we reap what we sow."

Because I desired to have a servant's heart and please God along with the leadership I was under, I buried my aspirations to push everyone else's vision, business, and dream for their life while my own slowly faded away. Please do not misunderstand what I'm attempting to convey. I am a firm believer living a life of servanthood, because nobody who achieved enormous feats did it solely on their own. People who accomplished greatness did it by standing on the shoulders of someone's vision they faithfully served. It's in the times of serving we are sowing good deeds that we will reap in our future. Aiding in someone else's vision is the time of refining, testing, and preparation to release what is inside of you. This is also a great opportunity to learn through mentorship by positioning yourself to receive the wisdom of someone who is laying your foundation that you will someday build on.

I have given my best to every leader I have been privileged to work under with a sincere heart and motive. I believe the time I have given to others hasn't been in vain. My heart is still to serve. So, I encourage you to ask God to reveal the people He has ordained for you to work under. Not only will that person or group of people pour their life into you, they will also have the foresight and know how to balance the work you are doing for their vision, with pushing you towards your own destiny.

Although I believe God's word that all things work together for my good, I still left class angry at myself for being so gullible. Why didn't it dawn on me to question any of the advice that was given to me? This is the reason why. Even if it didn't seem right or fair in my gut, the mere fact that the words came from a person of influence caused me to follow their path. I believed every teacher, authority figure, boss, and mentor I ever had in my life had my best interest at heart (I still actually believe that) so I trusted that they knew better than me. But now, here I am, forty-four years old suffering from dream amnesia. But, I purposed in my heart not to take this laying down. I took the anger I was feeling and used it as fuel to help me dig through the weeds of manipulation and bad counsel to find my dreams and rescue them from the coma they were in. It wouldn't have done any good aiming fiery darts at the people who said these things to me. Besides, some of the people weren't alive anymore or wouldn't recognize me if they saw me after thirty years, so why bother? All I desired was to dream again. And I was determined to breathe life back into my aspirations and no longer deny myself of being my authentic self.

I asked God for a strategy to recapture what had gotten away from me. The first thing that came to mind was to call my sisters. It made perfect sense, because they're nine, ten, and twelve years older than me. I figured they had memories of what I used to talk about when I was young, since I was quite the chatterbox in my youth like I am now. I asked them if they remembered what I used to speak about during my childhood. Thankfully, they were able to recall some of the things that I used to discuss. One of my sisters reminded me how much I loved sports. That began to jog my memory and took me back to my dream of wanting to be a sports medicine doctor or trainer for a professional football or basketball team. I was, and still am, a huge football fan. But, once I began to do the research and saw all of the science and biology classes I would have to take to be a doctor or trainer, that dream was short-lived, because I despise dealing with numbers.

Then, I went on to my next thing that gave my joy, that is talking and being heard. I went from wanting to care for professional athletes to wanting to major in broadcast journalism to become a famous talk show host on a FM gospel radio station, because I loved Jesus back then too. Or, I could see myself being the next Oprah Winfrey. I loved giving advice and being a voice that represented the people, as well as writing. I figured, if a chocolate girl of African descent, with some extra weight on her from the Midwest can pull it off, I can too with my personality. I started going in that direction by joining my high school's forensics and debate team that I won medals in my first year for oratory speech. I auditioned for a black history play for a community choir I was a part of for the first time, and landed one the starring roles as Mary McCloud Bethune. That's when I was exposed to monologues and recognizing my stage presence. I entered the Martin Luther King Jr. speech contest and won at my school the first time entering, which made me eligible to compete at the district level. I won that contest, so I moved to competing on the city-wide level and placed fourth. That was a big accomplishment for me, to get that far the very first time entering a competition in an arena I had no experience in.

Talking to them stimulated my memory to help me revisit my former self and remember my dreams. Not only did it put me back on the road to recovery, it gave me the revelation that what I wanted to do back in high school wasn't too far-fetched after all. I was wired and predestined to stand before people armed with a message of hope that will change their life. God put that dream in me. Being reminded of that by going back to such a sweet time in my life felt like taking the first deep breath after gasping for air, because I was mentally and emotionally choking. Not only did that journey fill me with the oxygen of grace to move forward in going after what was in my heart to do years ago, it taught me this valuable nugget of truth.

The Lesson Learned

No matter how big or ridiculous sounding your dream, goal, or vision may seem to others, remember this one thing, it's yours! Learn from my mistake and don't let anyone take your dream away from you. This attempt might come through people trying to talk you out of it or by making the fulfillment of their own dream more important than yours. You may have people in your life that are not able to dream as big as you, and that's ok. You owe it to yourself to get away from toxic people who think small, or try to make you feel bad for thinking big. Get surrounded by a support system that will encourage you to go after the greatness that's incubating inside of you, by laying a firm foundation for you to build on.

Recognize when someone is being manipulative by attempting to talk you out of what's in your heart. If they are trying to talk you out of it, can't see it in you, or if their motive is to keep you focused solely on their vision, consider that a red flag. If they make you feel wrong for dreaming, or if it violates your conscious, that is also a red flag. If you are neglecting your own dreams, gifts, and talents, or if they are lying dormant with no plan for them to be cultivated, the red flag is waving.

When you see these flags, take them as a warning sign and run. Just like you must be wise and protect yourself from being physically violated, you must safeguard your dreams and visions. Keep them away from those who will belittle, abuse, crush, or snatch them from you. There's True Freedom in discovering what's inside of you.

Personally, I believe healthy dreams come from God as seeds of greatness to be planted in the earth. Going after those dreams will fuel you to be great. Don't ever stop dreaming, because they will motivate you to keep you pressing through life's journey. Now, I'm up at night working on the God-given vision for my life and I'm having the greatest time ever. I encourage you to reach for your dreams. Fulfillment is waiting for you. How long will you keep it waiting?

Life Reflection Two

The serious medical condition I dealt with required me to go through two emergency surgeries within a forty-eight hour period. Because both procedures required a pretty large incision. I had to be "put under" both times. That wouldn't be a bad thing if a few years earlier I wouldn't have had my gallbladder removed and a hernia in my abdomen repaired within a year of each other. I also had to be unconscious for both of those surgeries. "That's several times to be knocked out in a such a short period," was my thought as I was being prepped for each operation. But the doctors assured me that my body could handle it, however I was still a little anxious about the whole procedure.

To be honest, every time I had to go through surgery I hated the thought and process of going under. The horror stories of mistakes being made, like people waking up in the middle of being cut open, plagued my mind. I hated the feeling and lack of control I had over what I did or said while trying to come out of that fog. I vaguely remember randomly yelling out my pastor's telephone number, so my family can call him to let him know I made it through the operation, all while I was in and out of consciousness. My poor husband caught the grunt of my altered state. When I woke up and discovered an empty room after one of the surgeries, I called my husband using all kinds of "F-bombs" which is totally out of character for me. I hardly have any memory of what I said. Faintly, I recall him saying, or better yet fussing, "Since when did you cuss like this? Never mind, go back to sleep, because you're still high!" I said all of that to say I'm not myself when I'm under sedation.

After waking up, I realized I had different I. V's from the ones I had before going under the knife. I had an eerie feeling and thought to myself I will never have a clue about everything that happened to me during those procedures. However, thankful is an understatement for how I felt knowing I made it through every time. I'm aware of the lurking possibility of never waking up again. Each time I laid on the surgery table and felt my body going to sleep, the reality of my mortality was thrown in my face. This was especially true since my heart had to be monitored due to the rate declining without warning constantly. I know it's cliché', but I started to think back over my life. Here I am in my early forties with a lot of life left in me to live for it to be possibly cut short. There's a whole world that I wanted to see, and places I wanted to go. I just started traveling the year before and had another trip planned that I was excited to go on. I knew there was a wellspring of untapped potential inside of me, and the possibilities for how far I could go in life was enormous. Now I'm finding myself in a position that I may not live to see who I had the potential of becoming.

In the best way I could, with all of the heavy medication that was in my system, I attempted to pray. I asked God to receive me if I didn't make it through this ordeal. I prayed that He would cover my daughters and comfort my husband if the unthinkable happened. My loved ones started flooding my heart, so I asked God to be with them too. Although I was pretty out of it, I could tell God was still hearing me. His peace began to flood my soul when I sensed my spirit connecting to Him. But, that was short lived when I had a real human moment in my thinking.

I began to think about everything in detail of what life could've been. My mind went to every book idea I never acted on. I started to recall all of the unwritten poems that I never got around to writing. Then, there were the business and ministry opportunities that I walked away from for a number of different reasons. To be truthful, let me call the reasons what they really are. They were excuses for dragging my feet on everything that was invested into me from the time I was a child.

I laid in that hospital with a great sense of remorse. I began to regret the fact that the grave site that my lifeless shell would occupy will have a wealth of witty and creative ideas that no one will ever benefit from, since they'll be buried with me. I was sorrowful for taking my legacy with me instead of leaving it behind for my children to gleam from. I knew in my heart there were people who needed my story that will never hear it, and I couldn't blame anyone but myself. With all of this going on in my mind, these words began to ring from my spirit. "God, If I don't make it, I'm sorry. Forgive me for everything You placed inside of me that will be buried along with me. I repent for not trusting You enough to step out on faith and follow the dream You had for my life. Forgive me for choosing to listen to people and ignoring Your leading. I'm sorry for not only disappointing You and the people You have ordained for me to impact, I repent for letting myself down. If You bring me out of this, I promise to shoot for the stars and utilize everything that You have placed inside of me, so Your will is done in my life. I vow to leave the earth realm empty from giving this life everything that I have. Please give me another chance to become who You have ordained for me to be."

Thankfully, God's grace stepped in and I was given another shot to get my life together and get my affairs in order. My life was spared so I can be about my Father's business. As I approach life this time around, I pledged to do so with a greater sense of urgency. I promised to move from thinking, wishing, and desiring things to putting my hand to the plow and putting the work in to turn my thoughts into reality. My new lease on life will not only benefit me, but everyone whose path this story will cross. My desire is to get moving and not allow the "what ifs" of failure to stop me ever again. It's sad that it took an experience like this to light a fire under me. However, I believed it happened this way for a reason and I'm grateful for it, because I walked away with a piece of wisdom to share.

The Lesson Learned

Each of us were predestined to be specifically wired with our own God-given gifts, talents, and abilities. But, how we use them has been left up to us. We were all put on earth for a reason, but it's up to us to discover the why behind our existence and walk out our destiny. Don't make the same mistake I made by assuming you have an unlimited time frame to go after your dreams. If you haven't noticed, you are getting older every day. Not too many people know how long the grace to achieve your God-given assignment will be present in your life, so stop making excuses and get moving. Don't procrastinate by making excuses. There will always be a reason why you shouldn't move towards fulfilling your purpose. If your mind is anything like mine, it's good for listing every argument concerning why you shouldn't do the things you've been called to do. Some of those reasons are valid like being outside of God's timing, or making sure your spouse is in agreement with you. It's always wise to make sure your house isn't divided so it will stand strong as you make moves.

Don't allow naysayers to stop you from tapping into the greatness that's inside of you. Meaning, everyone isn't going to understand or be excited for the dream that God has placed in you. It's not always easy to detect a pessimist, so ask God to enlighten your eyes. Soon, you will notice who will have something negative to say each time you begin to shine. You will take note when the same people begin to list the reasons why you can't achieve your dreams as opposed to finding ways to make it work. You will begin to recognize the stench of doubt and unbelief and crave the language of faith. Leave people alone who are not speaking the language of progression without any action of advancement.

Start where you are by surrounding yourself with like-minded people that will help you get to your divine destination. If they can't see it in you or if they're stuck themselves, they can't help you get there. If they are constantly looking at life through the rear-view mirror and always finding a reason why it can't be done, they can't help you get there. If they're making excuses for their own complacency or feel threatened by your potential, they can't help you get there. If there's no sense of urgency or drive to do what's inside of them, or if they're easily intimidated, they can't help you get there. If they lack the wisdom, knowledge, or foresight, they can't help you get there.

If it's in you write the book, start the business, or complete your education, and get the degree. Prepare yourself to purchase the home, compose the music, and record the CD. You have what it takes to submit the script, start the organization or ministry, and anything else that is in you to do. Love yourself enough to see the treasure that you are. Because there is True Freedom and fulfillment in tapping into the greatest resource that you have been given next to God Himself. That resource is YOU!

Life Reflection Three

The years 2014 through 2017 will go down in history as the season of challenge and transition for me. Hardly anything is the same as it was in years prior to this time frame. That's a huge statement for me, because I'm known for being a person whose life stays the same for the most part. Not only that, I loathe change. I hate change so much that my friends and loved ones have attempted to step in to help me "grow" in this area. They should know by now what they are in for when they make their attempts, but God bless them for their effort. My good sister-friend began to give me jewelry, so I can have a variety of accessories to choose from. This was her way to stop me from wearing the same shell set that I always choose that I have owned since the nineties. My husband recently "encouraged" me to throw away my tattered winter coat after fifteen years of literal wear and tear. With sadness, I submitted to his request after he said I look unloved in it. I've been talked about by my friends and family for carrying the same purse, wearing the same clothes, and keeping the same car until it falls apart. When I love, I love hard and it's difficult for me to let go. I have a ton of examples like this, but I'm sure you get the point.

My steady world as I knew it began to shift starting February 4, 2014. Ten years and six months after birthing my only child, I had my second child nine days before turning forty-one years old. I had a hard time re-adjusting to being a new mom. My body took longer to heal than it did ten years beforehand. As most new mothers are, I was tired. I suffered from postpartum depression that triggered thoughts of suicide. I even went as far as leaving my house in the middle of the night unannounced and took about six bottles of my husband's prescription medicine with me to swallow. I left my phone at home so I couldn't be found. I stared at those pills, but my oldest daughter's face kept flashing in front of me like a picture. Her image, along with the coaching of a dear friend, gave me the courage to return home without taking them. My erratic behavior scared my husband so bad that he called my doctor and pastor to get me the help I needed to come out of that dark place.

While this was going on, my mother's health was declining. She quickly went from this vibrant woman that was full of life and tenacity who raised me, to a fragile shell of herself that spent more time in the hospital and rehabilitation facilities than home. I hardly recognized her anymore. Her once sassy demeanor and sharp mind disappeared before my eyes. This is the same woman that worked two jobs before starting her own business to provide for her family. She was a concert promoter, president of a men's and women's pool league, and someone who broke so many barriers as a single African-American woman. She was well respected and a heavy hitter in her sphere of influence. She had a brilliant savvy and accomplished anything she put her mind to do.

My real-life superhero, who was known for fixing everything from cars to delicious cuisine, got to the point she could barely maneuver her hands. No words can describe the grief and devastation of watching my mother who was my last living parent slip away from me. September 19, 2014, she passed away. She left me with a little girl that just started middle school. My daughter was my mom's sidekick and they were crazy about each other. Now, I have to raise my girl without Grandma's love and support. She left me with a brand-new baby girl that wasn't old enough to have any memory of her. Since my older sister's children were already grown, I felt slighted for having to raise my babies without my mother like they had the chance to do.

At the same time, I was mourning for the loss of my mother, the place of employment that I loved was going through its own transition. The year before my mom's death, we moved into our third location in roughly three years. Up until building number three, the place I worked was a dream come true. We were free to set our own hours to come and go as we please. My boss was awesome to say the least. The workers and clients had a bond that was so special it was unreal. We laughed, cried, and shared our lives with each other in a way that very few experience in a job setting. All of us looked forward to coming to work every day, because we knew it was going to be a day full of fun, jokes, and creating sweet memories. But, when we moved into the third space, the rules and climate changed. She subleased a space inside of an already established business, so there were time restrictions and set hours that we could work.

The carefree environment that I once worked in became full of pressure and unease. Besides the cameras that monitored every move, I had a hard time adjusting to the new hours. Since I was the only one commuting a school-aged child back and forth to school, as well as taking care of a new baby, I couldn't be there early when the building opened to work early like the other workers did. My only option was working around my young family's schedule, so I usually ran over the time we were allowed to work. My frequent late nights became such a source of contention, the management outright snapped on me. I hated walking into that building. My predicament put my boss in an awkward position, because she felt caught in the middle of the tension. To put everyone at ease, I left the job that I loved after eleven years. I cried carrying out my belongings, because I knew in my heart that I will never work in an environment like that again.

Soon after I left my job, I received a call from my sister on an early Saturday morning. She told me she was on her way to see about our great-niece, because something happened to her. I immediately got a sick feeling. When the phone rang again, it was my sister. "I just identified her," are the words she said that I will never forget. She was stabbed to death. My niece was a beautiful twenty-six-year-old mother of two little girls. She was an exceptional young lady that was in the process of creating a children's clothing line. She was in school and had huge dreams. She made cornbread dressing and greens that tasted like she had a seventy-year-old soul. She had a huge heart and it's still hard to believe she's gone. Our family never lost a close family member by way of murder, so it shook everyone to the core. Because her trial is ongoing as I write this reflection, I can't mention anything about her alleged killer that was close to her and our family or the circumstances leading to her death. She continues to be greatly loved and missed while we are left to pick up the pieces.

Soon after my great-niece's death, things began to change at my church home. My first born was only a year old when we officially joined after visiting for over a year. The pastor was a man of integrity and had a huge heart. The congregation captured his vision for servanthood and followed his example of displaying God's love. That along with the awesome services and genuine concern for people made it easy to fall in love with the place. They were instrumental in saving my marriage when I was going to file for divorce. The children's ministry assisted in steering my daughter in the right direction. The ministry also gave me opportunities to develop my gifts and talents. They allowed me to write and recite poetry to complement the ministry's sermons. I was allotted numerous occasions to speak through leading prayers and even ministered a few sermons. They supported and prayed for me when I had speaking engagements outside of the church. He also promoted me to a leadership position and acknowledged the call of God on my life by granting me a minister's license.

As time went on, my desires began to change. I had a stronger desire to walk in the divine destiny I believe God has ordained for me. The more I came into a discovery and talked about the dream that was illuminating inside of me, the tension became more apparent with any move I made that hinted towards going in that direction. In their defense, I'll be the first to admit I made a lot of mistakes, blunders, and bad decisions on my journey to maturity. In fact, I nicknamed myself after Jesus' disciple who had the most to say, "Peter". Just like Peter, I had passion, drive, and a colorful personality. Peter and I had a lot in common but here's the thing that made us different. When the pressure was on, Peter walked away and denied who he was by denying Jesus. Denying who I am or what Christ has put inside of me to give the world will never be an option. It doesn't matter who wants to keep me boxed in or threatens to "pull back" or cut me off.

So, after much prayer and with an abundance of tears, my husband and I sensed in our hearts it was time to leave. I desired to do things in order by honoring the people who invested so much into my family and me personally. I attempted to give a notice of our intention to do things the right way by doing whatever it took to ensure a smooth transition with our departure. I'm releasing you now was the response I received. I sobbed during that call like I suffered a tragic loss. A prayer was said for me and my family during that call. When I hung up, it was a done deal. I wasn't allowed to hug or say my final goodbyes to the people I laughed, cried, labored with, and served with in ministry for a number of years.

My children couldn't go back to say goodbye to the friends they grew up with since they were toddlers. A decision was made that it was best for us to leave quietly, because I was known for being vocal and having a voice of influence with the congregation. An announcement being made after our departure would eliminate any emotional responses since we held such close ties with so many people. It also didn't give room for people to follow us by asking, "What church are you going to now?" My heart still hurts about the way things played out. But I wish them nothing but success and for God's will to be done in their life, because I still love them with a special place in my heart.

Now that I'm looking back at the series of events that took place during that time of my life in hindsight, I walked away with a wealth of valuable pieces of wisdom that I gathered.

The Lesson Learned

This was a time in my life that I struggled physically, financially, and emotionally in ways that I never would've imagined. I ate plenty of "humble pie" by borrowing money, asking for help from friends and family, and depending on others in ways I was never accustomed to. I know some of you can relate to what you're reading, because you cried the same tears of heartache. You yelled the same screams of rage from frustration that you could no longer hold. Chances are you had to walk away from places, things, and people that you once gave your best to. If you're like me, you pondered and tried to figure out if it's worth the hell you are going through, or if it's in you to move forward.

Here's the answer to that question; YES, IT IS! As long as you are among the living, there is life in you to be lived, dreams to go after, and God is not done with you. Personally, I had to learn to press through the pain and start to look at life for what it is and what I have now. I had to decide not to focus on who or what I'd lost. I encourage you to do the same, because constantly reliving those moments in your head will suck the life out of you. The grief from burying loved ones is real along with the pain of being rejected, betrayed, and lied on. The sting of being misunderstood, going through physical pain, and dealing with the aftermath of setbacks are real. So is saying goodbye to people you once held close to your heart.

However, just as real as the agony is, so is the ability to recover and still pursue your dreams. By rising from the ashes of sorrow, you will see there is life beyond the moment you may find yourself in. Now that I'm beyond the hard place where my life was falling apart, I can see how those things worked out for my good. Thank God things are coming together, and light is starting to emerge. I couldn't see it then, but now I realize why the goodbyes were necessary. I needed to let go and let a much-needed death of familiarity happen. Life depleting comfort zones that had the greatness incubating inside of me, gasping for air and nourishment, had to go. As a result of letting go, I've met lots of great people that are fanning the flame of my internal fire. They are speaking the same language of faith, living in the now, and preparing for tomorrow. I am surrounded by people who want to see me succeed, and if you let go of the pain, I believe the same thing can happen in your life.

If life happened to deal you a bad hand, turn the mess into a message that reaches your world to let them know you have what it takes to recover. Allow your life to be an example and refuse to let it punch you in the stomach without a response. Life can be a bully to the Clark Kent in you, but you don't have to let it take you out. Your inner superhero is waiting to come back with a one-two punch. Adorn your soul with a cape and matching boots that gives you the ability to fly. Decide to sail into the future. There's True Freedom in taking flight to soar into your destiny.

Having Healthy Relationships

Life Reflection One

September 16, 1996 was the day I married my best friend, love of my life, and the man of my dreams. He's everything that I want and need in a husband and I wouldn't change one thing about him or our marriage. That sounds good, doesn't it? "Good", is the picture a lot of people like to portray to the world (especially on social media) about their marriage and relationships in general. Often, this so-called picture is more of a smokescreen that's attempting to hide the painful reality of what's really going on in relationships. This happens in more than half of marriages, namely Christian unions. The world needs a real glimpse into a marriage journey instead of a facade of a stroll in the park. I'll be the first to admit we had our share of ups, downs, and challenges. Here's a real look at my battle wounds from the rocky start of our marriage journey.

My husband and I went to the same elementary school. He transferred to another school, so we didn't see each other again until we later reconnected during our high school years. We joined the same community organization that gave the city's youth an alternative to running the streets and being involved in the gang activity that was prevalent at that time. The option that was presented to us was the gospel of Jesus Christ. That also came with singing, dancing, acting, and traveling the nation with a spiritual family that is closely knitted to this day. We were friends for several years, but our brother/sister relationship made a switch. We started "secretly" dating at nineteen although we both had significant others at the time. We decided to keep it under wraps since neither of us wanted to hurt the people we were in relationships with. Neither did we want to break up with them. I know, our reasoning didn't make any sense.

At the time our feelings for each other started to grow, I was on the praise and worship team and he was a Sunday school teacher at the church that was connected to the association we were a part of. On top of accepting Jesus as Savior, and having committed relationships with other people, we committed to living a consecrated life of celibacy.

That vow we made was the life people thought we were conducting ourselves by. But the truth is we were living a double life. We depicted one thing, but behind closed doors we couldn't get enough of each other (yes, it's ok to read between the lines). After a while of being friends with benefits behind closed doors, we got sloppy keeping things hush-hush. The public sightings, sexual chemistry, and my change in demeanor were starting to become obvious to the spiritual saints that had a gift of reading people. A couple of the female adult mentors straight-out asked me what I was engaging in. The less aggressive woman that showed concern hinted around that she noticed behavior changes. I got away with denying it with her and she didn't press the issue, because she didn't know me as well.

However, there was another mentor that was a lot more assertive in her approach. She cornered me in a bathroom while church service was going on and demanded to know, "Who are you screwing, because your whole walk has changed along with your hips?" She proceeded to give me a tongue lashing for the ages. She reminded me that I was a virtuous young lady that had a mandate to possess my temple according to God's Word. She went on to quote what seemed like every scripture in the bible concerning sex outside of marriage. Her words convicted me, to the point of tears, about being a fornicator. Those feelings lasted until I left the church and met up with him that night.

A church family that wasn't afraid to get in each other's business for our own good, coupled with my new womanly curves, and a pregnancy scare exposed our nasty little secret. We were immediately removed from our positions (sat down in church terms), and we deserved it. Needless to say, the relationships with our other mates ended, especially since we all went to the same church. It was all a big mess, but at least we didn't have to be undercover anymore. Since there was nothing to hide anymore, we became an official couple and was open with our romantic union. That was bittersweet, although we were free to be together, there was no denying the condemnation we experienced from falling from our faith. Instead of us doing what we knew was right by attempting to make our wrongs right with God, we stopped going to church and moved in together.

We were in pure lust, but in our heart we knew our lifestyle was wrong. In our feeble attempt to do the right thing in our own way, we got engaged. It was better to marry to burn, right? Our pastor at the time told us that our marriage would not last a year, because anything that will take us out of God's will isn't in God's will for our life. He urged us to get our spiritual life in order before getting married. We didn't want to go through what seemed like a long process, all we wanted to do was get married. The pressure was also on to tie the knot, because of the promise we made my mother the day I told her I was leaving her house to move in with my boyfriend. She showed her disdain by telling me she didn't raise me to live in the house with "some man" that was not my husband. To calm her nerves and spare her the embarrassment of having a child that was shacking, we agreed that we will get married a year after we signed our lease. Without any pre-marital counseling or guidance, we got married at the courthouse despite our pastor's disapproval.

The honeymoon was short-lived, because we went and took each other through hell during our newlywed years. We hurt each other in ways that were unimaginable. The arguments were terrible and sometimes got violent. The hot sex life we had before marriage went ice cold so both of us broke our marriage vows and committed adultery. Divorce was brought up numerous times in those first few years, because both of us got to the point that we hated coming home. As a means of escape, I poured myself into my career, working fourteen-hour days at times to avoid home. Although we wanted to call it quits, I remembered the words that my pastor spoke. I was determined to prove him wrong. Besides, there was something inside of both of us that wouldn't allow us to walk away. Even though the hard times were mentally and emotionally draining, there were some good times we shared that we could reflect on. Neither of us wanted to start over, so in a last stitch effort to salvage what looked like a hopeless situation, we decided to try marital counseling. We went to a pastor that we both knew we could trust, that didn't know us very well to get non-biased counsel. We also didn't want to hear the I told you so's from our former pastor.

Once the pastor heard both of our concerns and asked us a series of questions, he did two things that changed my life. He told us what our main issue was, that should've been common sense. We were endeavoring to live a life of covenant without the God of our covenant. We sheepishly admitted that we haven't been to any church in nine years at that time. Instead of him becoming judgmental, he graciously asked us to bow our heads right there in his office and prayed for us. That moment we made the decision to give our life back to the Lord and accept Him as Savior. After he made sure our spiritual life was back in order, he addressed the next major issue. We lacked the practical tools for a successful marriage. Both of us came from homes of divorced parents and we didn't have one example of a successful marriage that we could learn from at that point. We were trying to learn as we go and that was a huge mistake. Five years into our marriage, we got the pre-marital counseling that we didn't get at the beginning. Once we were properly equipped with what we needed, we managed to pick up the pieces to save our marriage. At the time of writing this reflection, we're looking forward to celebrating twenty-two years of a strong marriage rooted in love. My marriage journey taught me some valuable truths.

The Lesson Learned

In spite of the romanticized image and hype behind the dream, marriage in and of itself is not a picture-perfect fairytale of living happily ever after. The reality of married life begins soon after the high of that great day of celebration is over. Not to sound cliché, but there's a lot of work that's involved in building a successful marriage, because the exchange of "I do's" does not automatically make you one with your mate. The process of bonding comes along with ups and downs along the journey. That's why it's vital to get equipped with tools of success so you will be able to weather any season of marriage you may find yourself in.

Do yourself a favor; don't go through what we endured. Get help before the storm hits, because it's coming. No marriage is immune from it. It doesn't matter how spiritual you are, or your mate is. It takes effort for two different people that had their own life experiences, share of hurts, and views of life to become one. To make the necessary adjustments for it to happen in the smoothest way possible, it's best to have pre-marital counseling from someone who has wisdom and a good marriage before your wedding day. But, if you've already jumped in like I did without preparation, it isn't too late to seek help at any stage of your marriage. Find good role models that mirror the kind of union you envision for yourself and get equipped with tools for success.

Most important, include Christ in your relationship. The biggest mistake we made was getting away from the foundation that we originally built our lives on. We eventually made it back to our first love, but not without learning that lesson the hard way. Although my husband and I had a turbulent beginning, I'm thankful that we didn't abort the mission. Now, we can truly celebrate over 21 years of falling in, out, and back in love with each other. We had to decide to work at our marriage and not give up. If you make the same commitment and to stick to it, I believe your relationship can be saved and survive those tough seasons. But, you must be willing to change, make adjustments, accommodate, and be mindful of each other's needs.

To be honest, we could've avoided a lot of painful moments if we would've been equipped beforehand and kept God in our union. Our journey taught us there's True Freedom in staying the course through perseverance and endurance, because there's a sweet victory that awaits on the other side for you. How long will you keep your victory waiting?

Life Reflection Two

I always loved playing with my hair during my teen years and wanted to style my friend's hair every chance I had. My love affair with Hair didn't start there. When I was a child, Barbie didn't have enough hair for me to play with. So, every Christmas I got a deluxe doll head that came with beauty supplies to give me a full make-believe salon experience. That was the only doll I ever wanted each year. My poor mother went through extreme measures to make sure I had a fresh head since I practically combed my doll's hair until she was bald.

Amazon Prime didn't exist in the seventies or eighties, so mail ordering toys was a big deal. She never failed to soothe my fix year after year since combing hair became my high. This went on throughout my childhood. When I went to beauty school instead of a four-year college, none of my friends and family were surprised. Once I graduated, I passed the State Board Exam on the first attempt. I was Twenty-two years old in May of 1995 when I became a licensed cosmetologist. Over that time span, I've met some amazing people that I grew life-long bonds with. I have relationships with multiple generations of women within families. I built a full clientele through word of mouth without any advertising. My career has been awesome for the most part.

Along with the joys that came with being a hairdresser, life in the beauty industry also has a tremendous amount of pressure and sacrifice. Like most stylists and barbers that put themselves, their children, relationships, and life itself on the back burner for the sake of being available for their clientele, I was no acceptation. I missed both of my daughter's monumental moments, like first time rolling over, crawling, and taking steps. Since my birthday is the day before Valentine's Day, I spent most of them at work, because women want to be cute for the date night. There were countless family events I missed. Not to mention working while tired, in pain, or dealing with my own stress as I listen to everyone else's problems with a smile on my face. Chances are, I was probably hungry too. I honestly don't believe the average client has a clue what a dedicated stylist gives up for the sake of pleasing them. I say that because when we step away from "the chair" for any reason that range from maternity or medical leave, the death of a loved one, vacation (that we need too) or to enjoy life, someone isn't happy about it. From my personal experience, I've been harassed while away through text messages, inboxes through social media, and telephone calls that don't seem to go away regardless of the circumstance. I even had a client ask me if I was coming to work the day after my mother died.

Then, there are the clients who have no idea what personal time or space is. They will call or text as late as after midnight, during Sunday Morning Church Service, and worse of all, my Sabbath Monday. They think nothing of it like it's their right to disturb my personal and family time. Spending time with Jesus isn't as important as making a hair appointment either. Some of them are convinced that my world revolves around them and all I have to think about is their hair. My clients are like that, because it's mostly my fault. I always strived to give every person that sits in my chair a personal experience. Because I'm so chummy with them, they've become quite comfortable with me. I don't take the relationships I have with them for granted, so I engage and talk to them with a genuine heart. By the time they leave, not only do they have a new hairdo, they have a good friend they can confide in. Doing that over the course of multiple years got the lines blurred. I understand where I went wrong, so I tolerated it along with being taken on guilt trips, and pressured into cutting times away short because, "You know I have an event coming up and I don't trust anyone else to do my hair." I heard that phrase so many times I should get it tattooed on me.

In past times, I caved under pressure by cutting medical and maternity leaves short and returning to work regardless of how I felt physically or my personal feelings. Since I'm self-employed and didn't have disability benefits, I didn't want to risk losing a client when they threatened to go somewhere else to be serviced. I dealt with a lot of mental warfare worrying about the clients that had attitudes, because I decided to take care of my family or me. When I had a medical emergency that put my life in danger, I was forced to approach my recovery different this time. Although the pressure was on a whole new level, I refused to buckle.

On top of taking a few months off from a high demand clientele without notice, I had to relinquish my responsibilities of being the Operation's Manager of the salon. My partners depend on me to oversee the hairdressers as well as upkeep the building. I stood firm on my decision to fully recover and didn't rush the process before the smock came back on. I didn't focus or give any attention to the people who didn't like or respect it. To my surprise, I came back to grateful and more important a patient clientele that was glad to see me. I had a couple of people that were antsy, but it wasn't anything close to what I experienced in past times. One of my favorite clients went out her way to drop money off at my home to help cover unexpected expenses. Another one of my favorites came to the salon with roses to show her love and appreciation. My career in the service industry has taught me a lot about relationships.

The Lesson Learned

People will take their cues and treat you according to the tone that you set. If you fail to set boundaries, people will act as if you don't have any. They will do what's considered acceptable in their eyes, simply because you haven't drawn any lines or set any rules for them to follow. You must set a climate that teaches people how to respect and honor you or run the risk of it not happening. This happens by prioritizing your values and letting them be known. This doesn't have to be done in a mean or malicious manner. You can gently convey your heart and decide to be consistent with the system that has been put in place. People will rise to the standard that you set. Don't get me wrong; I still have people that try to contact me outside of my regular business hours, because people will still try you. I no longer mask my anger and answer the call or respond to a message outside of normal business hours while pretending to be fine with the interruption.

When teaching people how to treat you, there's also another side that comes with speaking up. That aspect is hearing with attentiveness. Keep yourself open to listening to someone's heart concerning a matter. This can come in every form from constructive criticism done in love, to flat out insults that were designed to discount your self-worth. No matter what form it may come in, there's always something that can be learned that will position you to make adjustments for your betterment. Taking in criticism isn't always easy. In fact, it can hurt when you are trying to put your best foot forward. When you can be mature enough to put your personal feelings aside and use those comments as fuel for your advancement, you will be better off in the long run.

Avoid making the mistakes that I made and know it's ok to let people know how you feel or what the truth is behind saying no. Don't allow people to take advantage or misuse you. No is not a bad word, although I had trouble saying it for years. It came from the fear of disappointing or upsetting someone along with the fear of rejection. You can do it in a way that will not be offensive. I had to learn to give people a realistic scenario instead of trying to be a superhero by over obligating myself to "save the day". I ended up with angry clients who were in the salon longer than they wanted to be, so my efforts of trying to please everyone backfired when nobody was happy at the end of the day. Saying no to my clients that had a habit of making last-minute appointments, taught them to call in advance to ensure they will be able to get an appointment with me. Not only are my clients a lot happier because they are being serviced more efficiently, I'm working under less pressure and stress.

Isn't that what relationships are all about? It's all about communication. The better we get at communicating, the more enriched our relationships will be. There's True Freedom in having healthy relationships whether they're professional, ministry related, or personal.

Life Reflection Three

Before I go into this reflection, allow me to explain myself for the sake of my loved ones and close friends that might be reading this. I admit that I have fallen short with spending quality time with the people who mean the most to me over the years. For that, I give you all my sincerest apologies. Recently, I've attempted to do better by attending family events and making myself more available for my sister/friends. So, please don't roll your eyes because you recall the times I didn't show up at different functions or respond to the daily text messages or social media tags. Please know that I love you and I'm growing in this area, ok?

Anyone who knows me can attest that I am a true extrovert that values people and relationships of all sorts. I love connecting with people, because I thrive on the energy it gives me, a lot like the oxygen that I breathe. I'm in my element when I'm connecting to and bonding with someone. As far back as I can remember, I've always been this way. My personality is quite bubbly, so I'm known for being a people magnet, because it doesn't take long to notice me when I enter a room. Not that I'm gloating or trying to showboat, I'm a vocal person by nature and come from a long line of showy people. It comes from a sincere place, since I have a huge heart that loves hard. When I enter into a relationship, I never think it might be short term or for a temporary season. I have the tendency of having a long-term mentality when it comes to relationships. A prime example of this is knowing although my daughter is in high school, I still keep in touch with the pre-school and elementary school staff from her old schools. I'm still friends with my best friend that I met in kindergarten.

My approach towards relationships have been a great way to stay connected to so many special people I've met over the years. But on the other hand, it continues to be a great source of tremendous pain that's difficult to shake at times. My feelings have been crushed by friends, authority figures, and family members that I love dearly, because they've cut me off, pulled back, and acted as if we were never close at one point. One of my greatest personality flaws that I'm working on is my inability to handle rejection and let people go when they walk away. The main reason this is a challenge for me is due to my belief in putting the work in to make a relationship successful. Personally, I believe it's a cop-out to end a relationship and cut ties with someone over trivial matters that can be resolved with a plan and adjustments. Especially if you call yourself a believer or a person of faith. How can it be justified to operate in such an ungodly manner when there's no example of Jesus handling people that way in scripture? What if God treated you like you treat others? Would you even have a savior or would He have cut you off by now?

(Side note) Please don't take what I'm conveying out of content. I'm not talking about staying in a dangerous relationship regardless of the circumstances. If a relationship of any kind is mentally or physically abusive, please seek help and make sure you're safe. When a situation becomes continually toxic with behavior that's attacking you or the people that are connected to you like your children, please use wisdom and take measures to assure everyone's safety that is involved.

I had a particular friend that I've known since my teen years. When I first met her, I quickly grew an admiration for her, because she was mature in spiritual matters. She was an eloquent speaker and was gifted in a number of areas. Years later, our friendship grew closer and we began to spend more time together. We shared secrets, prayed together, and treated each other like real sisters. We argued, made up, protected each other, and spent time with each other's families to the point it became expected to be at each other's family events. We even slept at each other's house. It was a great friendship that I valued a great deal.

One day, I noticed that her husband blocked me on social media (she didn't have a page that I knew of). When I asked if there was anything we needed to talk about, I was blown off, ignored, and flat out rejected. I thought we had enough repour built to be able to talk and resolve whatever it was she was obviously offended about. I would walk in a room, she would go the other way. I would say hello and she suddenly went deaf. The disdain she had for me was so bad, she refused to accept or reach out for my help when I know she needed it. Now, that's a grudge for the ages. This went on for a number of years.

Over those years I tried my best to reconcile with her, because I couldn't accept that she suddenly didn't want to be bothered with me anymore. Her cutting me off was bad enough, but not having a clue why it happened tormented me. Not having closure was a sore spot for me and a source of tremendous pain, so I kept trying. I asked her numerous times if we could talk. She flat out refused. I even asked someone I knew she respected to mediate for us, and she refused that approach. Since we had the same circle of friends, it made the situation that much harder to deal with, because they were caught in the middle of the foolishness of having to choose who to spend time with. Finally, after years of fighting a losing battle, I gave up on trying to salvage our friendship. I walked away from everything and everyone that connected us together on a regular basis.

Soon (only a few months) after I threw in the towel, I received a call notifying me that she passed away. I didn't want to believe she was gone. Not only did I mourn her loss, I also grieved over all of those wasted years of contention between us. Was it worth the nonsense? Looking back at everything that took place, that's exactly what it was, nonsense. Now I have no choice but move forward with my life. I had to make a decision to be at peace, because I know I did everything I could to reconnect with her. I had to tell myself to focus on the good things and the multiple sweet memories I have of her and laughs we shared, because she was my bestie at one point. For whatever reason, we weren't connected the last years of her life, I have to live the remainder of my life without the closure of us having "that talk." I still tried to honor her in death by beginning chapter forty-five of my life (my birthday) on a bittersweet note. I went to a choir rehearsal to sing at her homegoing celebration and did some other things in her honor. Although it's a painful reality to live with, I gained some insight about the whole ordeal.

The Lesson Learned

Life is too short to live in regret, bitterness, or allow circumstances to hinder us from having healthy relationships with the people we love. We are all flawed humans with hang-ups and shortcomings. It should be expected that we get on each other's nerves from time to time. But if we can see each other the way God sees us, it will give us the patience and tenacity we need to walk in His love and reflect it on each other. A relationship doesn't have to end or be completely "cut off" even if it evolves during different stages of life and different seasons. Make every effort to stay connected and reconcile with the people in your life that are estranged from you. One day all of us are going to stand before God and give an account for our life and how we treated His people. What report will you have to give?

Because life is short, don't waste your time chasing after the people who don't value you enough to see your real worth. I spent a lot of time trying to appease my so-called friends and other people who just didn't have the insight of the gem they possessed in having me in their life. I'm not saying this out of vanity. Because God said, "I am fearfully and wonderfully made," I can say that with confidence. Once that became real to me, it began the new celebration of me. I had to learn to thank God for myself and explore the woman behind the many titles that I carry to serve other people. I had to realize it was time to have a love affair with her, because frankly I find my inner me quite intriguing. I encourage you to do the same. Fall in love with the core of who you are and let people go who don't embrace who you are. It's time for you to emerge, evolve, and step out for the world to see the beautiful creation that you are. I had to make up my mind to no longer second guess myself or be self-conscious about what anyone thought of me other than God.

Allow this to be the start of having a new focus on the sweet side of life. Aim to be the best you that you can be by loving yourself enough to realize the treasure you are. Make the adjustments to spend more time with friends and family that actually wants you in their life. If someone has to go as far as contemplating whether they want you in their life, they are not worth the time, effort, and/or investment of what you have to offer. Spend more time with yourself, and most importantly, gain a deeper understanding of the God who created you in His image. There's True Freedom in new beginnings and having a healthy relationship with yourself.

Conclusion

I pray you were blessed by reading a sample of Transparent Moments. Hopefully, you can apply some of the practical tips to your life by learning from my bad decisions and life lessons. I desire to share Transparent Moments with you for a few reasons. One, we live in a world where it's possible to have over ten thousand friends on social media, yet dwell in a state of isolation. Countless people feel as if nobody understands or can relate to what they are going through. What I am attempting to do is bring assurance that you are not alone. The battle that you are facing doesn't have to be fought alone. There's nothing new under the sun; so, someone has been where you are in life. Help is available to assist you in overcoming the obstacle or struggle you are up against. More important, there are still good people in the world that wants to see you walk in victory and is willing to give you the keys to success.

Second, I believe that everyone doesn't have to learn the hard way by going through actual trials like I did during the first half of my life. Some pitfalls can be avoided by learning from other people's mistakes. I want the lessons that I learned to help you live a better life. It's my desire to see people walk in the liberty that is available to you. Lastly, I hope this will inspire you to write your own story to release the superhero that's inside of you. We all have one. If I can do it, so can you.

Look for a full collection of Transparent Moments to be released, as well as a full array of books and other material from the True Freedom Connection Series. Look for The True Freedom Connection Network and website that is also on the horizon. This organization endeavors to unite a divided world by showing people we all have things in common that will bond us as a human race, as we help each other live a better life.

Printed in the United States
By Bookmasters